C000217728

MY FLOWER GARDEN

Agatha Christie

Illustrated by Richard Allen

SOUVENIR PRESS

THERE is no knowing
What time shall bring,

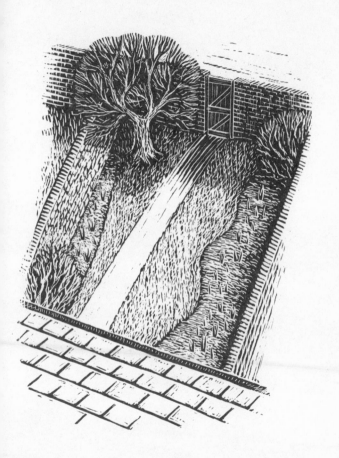

WHAT then is growing
This day of Spring?

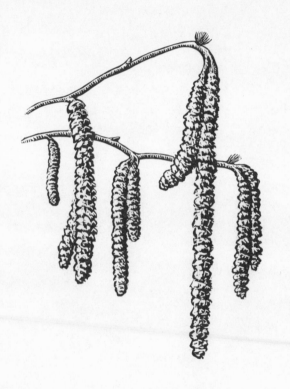

LOVE that is lonely,
Love far away,

AH! could I only
See you for a day.

Love-that-lies-bleeding

A<small>ND</small> love-in-the-mist,

TULIPS that need you
Still staying unkist.

YOU are my heart, love,
And you are my life,

WE are apart, love,
And I am your wife.

GOD then have pity
And bring you to me

Here in the city

FROM over the sea.

WHEN you come home, love,
What words will there be?

Y<small>OU</small> will say 'Sunflower'

And say it to me.

Photoset and Printed in Great Britain by
Redwood Burn Limited, Trowbridge, Wiltshire